ISBN: 9781096388753
Independently published

DEDICATION

To Nirvani, Ryan, Sam and the kids at Grange Primary School, Ealing. We've learned so much from you all. Keep using your strengths to shine every day.

To Maureen and Michael Mullally who practiced strengths-based parenting though they didn't know it's name. They truly understood the uniqueness of their four children and nurtured us and our individual talents with love and kindness. Thank you both for never pushing me to be anything other than myself. The strengths I admire most in you mum are self-control, curiosity, gratitude and perseverance. Rest in peace dad, your strengths of humility, honesty, spirituality, prudence and love remain with me forever.

GRATITUDE

We are indebted to all the positive psychology leaders and researchers, too numerous to mention but most especially Martin Seligman, Ryan Niemiec and VIA (viacharacter.org) on which this book is based. Thank you also to our families for your on-going support especially Dr. Ann Mullally, Jane Mullally and Dr and Mrs Saha.

ABOUT THE AUTHORS

Mary Ellen Saha BSc. BA. MA. LCH Dip

Mary Ellen is an educator, parent coach and career coach. She has qualifications in Psychology, Positive Psychology, Coaching, Kids Mindfulness and Character Strengths. She runs *Mindful Strengths* after school clubs in West London. Mary Ellen's top strengths are Love, Love of Learning, Zest, Hope, Forgiveness, Wonderment, Creativity, Curiosity, Gratitude and Honesty. She loves running and yoga!

Anirban Saha BSc MRes. BSoM Dip

Anirban is a trainer and meditation teacher. He has qualifications in Meditation, Chemistry and Molecular Engineering. He runs meditation courses for adults. Anirban's top strengths are Judgement, Hope, Gratitude, Love, Wonderment, Prudence, Creativity, Fairness, Honesty, and Humour. He also loves sci-fi and skateboarding!

INTRODUCTION

We created our company FUTR NOW, to teach kids and adults mental well-being life skills to counter the overwhelming negativity in our frenetic world. We noticed the stress of modern life with its busy 'doing' attitude and constant connecting and comparing via technology was having a detrimental impact on the mental health of kids and adults around us in our home city, London. Social comparison and anxiety about our kid's future seems to have reached a feverish pitch. Testing, tutoring, rushing, pushing and scheduling of kids are normal in the city we live in and most cities around the world today.

Many parents conform to this pattern because they are either too exhausted or too scared to try anything else. It's understandable in a world that is on 24/7. Working and parenting with this 'busy-busy' mindset is often depleting and divisive. Parents are constantly in reacting mode, scanning the horizon for bad news about the world, work and kids and so arming themselves in anger and defensiveness. This regularly leads to arguments both at work and at home. This anxiety is both contagious and self-fulfilling. As humans we have a negativity bias and so seeing our kids and our lives through this negative filter happens automatically and all too easily. Fear wins every time and we stay stuck on the wheel like the proverbial hamster.

FUTR NOW presents another way - An optimistic FUTURE firmly rooted in the HERE and NOW.

HERE we learn how to turn away from the *external* fast-paced-rat-race and open our eyes to the *internal* - to our true selves and our kids as they *are* in this present moment, huffs and tantrums included! We train ourselves to tune into their STRENGTHS rather than their test scores. We acknowledge their small everyday joys rather than planning out their prescribed futures.

HERE we enable kids and adults to focus on the *good stuff,* our STRENGTHS within. We seek self-awareness in the NOW. We learn what 'being' rather than 'doing' feels like. We train ourselves to enjoy silence. We foster an accepting attitude.

HERE pausing becomes habitual, gratitude abounds, kindness triumphs, empathy thrives and appreciation of STRENGTHS is the new normal.

GUIDELINES

How, Who, What, When, Where & Why?

HOW
Discover your top strengths by following these steps.

i) Complete the LIFT ME UP Exercise together (Parent and Kid), found at the end of these guidelines and write answers in the spaces provided.

ii) Complete the strengths survey with your kid. Go to http://futrnow.pro.viasurvey.org (link is on futrnow.org) The survey is free and it takes 10 minutes. Also it's fun! First register with an adult email address. Once you've registered there is an option to select which survey- adult or youth. Select youth and complete; you'll then receive an email with a link to the results. Be sure you complete the adult survey too. You can log back in at any time to view both results.

iii) Colour in your top 5 strengths on the My Strengths page. Next chat about the results together. What strengths do you have in common with your kid? What strengths are unique to you?

iv) Strengths Pages: There are 24 character strengths in alphabetical order. Each strength has two pages.

Colour-in Page : The first page is the colour in page, with a cartoon of us and a definition of the strength. You can cut out this page and your kid can colour it in and stick it up at home, especially if it's one of their top strengths. Use this page to become familiar with the strengths name. Use the definition as a starting point for conversation with your kid. Do you agree with this description? How would you describe this strength in your own words?

Action Page : The second page goes deeper. It has five segments; Spot it, Stretch it, Superstars, Screentime and Songs. Each segment is intended as a starting point for a conversation with your kid.

SPOT IT summarises how you can spot this strength in your kid and how they can spot it in others. Use this section to become familiar with *under-use*, *over-use* and *ideal-use* of a strength. Again try to be open minded about definitions here. The optimum level will differ for each kid and adult. The secret to super strengths use is to be aware of when and where to turn a strength up or down.

STRETCH IT involves reflection and action exercises. Using the spaces provided your kid can write their strengths story. Perhaps the adult can share their strengths story verbally first.

SUPERSTARS lists people who embody this strength. Some you may have heard of, some you may have not.

SCREENTIME lists TV shows, and films that have characters that embody this strength, many fictional some autobiographical. Also included are choices where the main characters *under-use* and *over-use* this strength.

SONGS lists music that exemplifies the strength or it's over use or under use. Note these lists are not exhaustive and encourage your kid to add their own superstars, films, shows and songs in the spaces provided

WHO

This book designed for kids aged ten upwards. The examples listed in Superstars, Screentime and Songs are subjective. Please use due diligence to decide if these are suitable for your kid. Each kid is unique. We have not given age guidelines for any films, TV or songs as we believe you know best. These lists are merely an invitation to start a conversation with your kid. Use blank spaces provided to add to these lists.

WHAT

The exercises in this book are based on scientific research from the last twenty years, particularly on Character Strengths and Virtues: A Handbook and Classification (CSV) by Christopher Peterson & Martin Seligman. The CSV classifies 24 strengths under six broad virtues that consistently appear across history and culture; wisdom, courage, humanity, justice, temperance and transcendence. Previous to this 2004 publication there were only reference books on mental illness. Widely used in USA is the Diagnostic and Statistical Manual of Mental Disorders (DSM-5). In the UK we use the International Classification of Diseases, (ICM-10). Whereas these manuals catalogue mental illness, the CSV is a catalogue of mental well-being (strengths). The CSV is part of a larger effort of positive psychology research and practice to not just enable kids and adults to overcome their disorders but to understand and better realise their strengths and therefore flourish. Research shows that when adults and kids focus on their strengths this has a lasting effect on their mental well-being and happiness. This effect is true for those who are mentally unwell as well as for those 'doing ok' but seeking a more optimistic, flourishing and fulfilling life. The research shows that if you focus on your strengths you can live a happier life no matter what your current circumstances or family history. Research also shows that across all countries *the* one common factor that increases happiness are good relationships. As Christopher Peterson summarised – *people matter*. The key to good relationships is appreciating each other's strengths.

WHEN

When Can You Use Your Strengths?
Anytime for anything! See if you can become a family who notices strengths use every

day and applauds each other for using strengths to do many tasks at home, e.g. homework (perseverance, creativity, kindness, curiosity), washing up dishes (zest, teamwork) , getting ready for bed, school, classes/activities (prudence, leadership, self-control, hope), family meals (gratitude, curiosity, creativity) family games (forgiveness, fairness, judgement, bravery, empathy) and family travel (point of view, teamwork, spirituality, humour). Why not divide up family chores with strengths?

WHERE

We suggest your kid cuts out and colours-in their top 5 strengths, then pin the five sheets up in their bedroom, playroom, study area or family notice board.

WHY

Why is it a good idea for kids and adults to know and grow their strengths?

Using your strengths is scientifically proven to boost confidence, reduce stress, manage problems, accomplish goals, strengthen relationships and increase happiness. Check out the strengths video here: futrnow.org/about

LIFT ME UP EXERCISE

Write down the first answer that comes to mind in the spaces opposite.

Learning - What subject have you learned easily at school or home?

Instinct - What activity are you looking forward to tomorrow?

Focus - What subject, sport or craft do you find it easy to concentrate on?

True Grit - Which activities do you persevere with in spite of set-backs?

Merit - Which actions have you been praised for by teachers or parents?

Energy - What are you doing when you are energised and you feel like you can keep going forever?

Uniqueness - What activities do ONLY YOU seem to enjoy doing?

Priority - What activity do you do first thing each day? Or what do you never forget to do?

LIFT ME UP EXERCISE

Child Answers

L _____

I _____

F _____

T _____

M _____

E _____

U _____

P _____

Adult Answers

L _____

I _____

F _____

T _____

M _____

E _____

U _____

P _____

BRAVERY

I STAND UP FOR WHAT I BELIEVE IS RIGHT.

Remember to check out the FUTR NOW **YouTube** Channel where all the Strengths SONGS listed in this book can be found in our handy STRENGTHS SONGS PLAYLISTS from Bravery to Zest. Find the YouTube links at futrnow.org

We'd love to hear your feedback. Please email here@futrnow.org with your suggestions for Superstars, Screentime and Songs!

BRAVERY

This person challenges the norm. This person raises their hand and speaks up in large groups. OVERUSE = Carelessness. UNDERUSE = Cowardice. IDEAL USE = Facing fears and hardships head on.

i) Write about a time when this strength really energised you. ii) List all the times/activities when you used this strength last week. iii) List what stopped you using this strength last week. iv) List ways you can use this strengths to overcome difficulties this week. Take one action today. v) Throughout your day PAUSE before you speak and act. Ask yourself, "Is what I'm about to do a reflection of who I am and what I want to be? Discuss each evening with a parent how it went.

Molly Craig (Kelly), Iqbal Masih, Las Brujas skaters, Ryan White, Sarinya Srisakul, Bob Marley, Luo Dengping, Aisholpan Nurgaiv, Claudette Colvin, Nancy Wake, Professor Green, Nadezhda Popova, Angelina Jolie, Serafina Battaglia

Supergirl (TV), Lost Song, The Hollow (TV), Harry Potter Films, The Breadwinner, Moana, Alice in Wonderland, Spirited Away, Star Wars: The Last Jedi, Incredibles Films, Willow, Good Will Hunting, Whale Rider, The Sound of Music, Casablanca, Indiana Jones Films, Batman Begins, Apollo 13, Cool Hand Luke, Rebel Without A Cause.

SONGS

Rabbit Heart - Florence & The Machine, Get Up Stand Up - Bob Marley, Can't Hold Us Down - Christina Aguilera, F.E.A.R. - Ian Brown, Survivor - Destiny's Child, Roar - Katy Perry, Every Breaking Wave - U2, Lullaby - Professor Green, Fear Of The Dark - Iron Maiden, I Can – Nas, My Way – Frank Sinatra, Stand Up and Be Strong – Keb Mo

TODAY'S DATE _____

MY STRETCH IT ANSWERS

MY SUPERSTARS

MY SCREEN TIME

MY SONGS LIST

Remember to check out the FUTR NOW **YouTube** Channel where all the Strengths SONGS listed in this book can be found in our handy STRENGTHS SONGS PLAYLISTS from Bravery to Zest. Find the YouTube links at futrnow.org

We'd love to hear your feedback. Please email here@futrnow.org with your suggestions for Superstars, Screentime and Songs!

CREATIVITY SPOT IT

This person shares new ideas, brainstorms easily and quickly. This person sees and does things in a unique way. OVERUSE = Eccentricity. UNDERUSE = Conformity. IDEAL USE = Flexible Originality

STRETCH IT

i) Write about a time when this strength really energised you. ii) List all the times/activities when you used this strength last week. iii) List what stopped you using this strength last week. iv) List ways you can use this strengths to overcome difficulties this week. Take one action today. v) Throughout your day PAUSE before you speak and act. Ask yourself, "Is what I'm about to do a reflection of who I am and what I want to be? Discuss each evening with a parent how it went.

SUPERSTARS

Wislawa Szymborska, Lubaina Himid, Kate Bush, The Beatles, Banksy, Justice (Duo), Bridget Riley, Tori Amos, Chimamanda Ngozi Adichie, Picasso, Selda Bagcan, Jay Z, Charlie Booker, Vivienne Westwood, Bjork, Leonard Cohen, St Vincent, Heston Blumenthal, Katy Perry, Violeta Parra, Jenny Holzer, Tamara De Lempicka

SCREENTIME

Chef's Table, Art Ninja, Junior Bake Off, Dr Who, Labyrinth, Back To The Future, Sing Street, Annedroids, Lego films, Ratatouille, Cloudy with a Chance of Meatballs, Unikitty, Yo Kai Watch, Gnomeo & Juliet, Loving Vincent

SONGS

Bohemian Rhapsody - Queen, Supermagic - Mos Def, Portrait of a Masterpiece - The D.O.C., Brenda's Got A Baby - Tupac, King's Dead - Jay Rock, Kendrick Lamar, Future & James Blake, Malamente –Rosalía, Magical Mystery Tour - The Beatles, Ziggy Stardust - David Bowie, Human Behaviour - Bjork, Heavy Metal-Justice, Jacuzzi Rollercoaster - Róisín Murphy, Free Yourself - The Chemical Brothers, Algorithm - Muse, Apeshit - The Carters, Electric Feel – MGMT

TODAY'S DATE ----------

MY STRETCH iT ANSWERS

MY SUPERSTARS

MY SCREEN TiME

MY SONGS LiST

Remember to check out the FUTR NOW **YouTube** Channel where all the Strengths SONGS listed in this book can be found in our handy STRENGTHS SONGS PLAYLISTS from Bravery to Zest. Find the YouTube links at futrnow.org

We'd love to hear your feedback. Please email here@futrnow.org with your suggestions for Superstars, Screentime and Songs!

CURIOSITY

SPOT iT

This person asks questions frequently. This person displays awareness of their environment and comments on their surroundings, noticing objects, clothing, art and details. OVERUSE = Being nosey. UNDERUSE = Disinterest. IDEAL USE = Exploring and experimenting

STRETCH iT

i) Write about a time when this strength really energised you. ii) List all the times/activities when you used this strength last week. iii) List what stopped you using this strength last week. iv) List ways you can use this strengths to overcome difficulties this week. Take one action today. v) Throughout your day PAUSE before you speak and act. Ask yourself, "Is what I'm about to do a reflection of who I am and what I want to be? Discuss each evening with a parent how it went..

SUPERSTARS

Vivian Maier, Madonna, Prof Brian Cox, Brenda Milner, Elena Favilli, Dan Buettner, Todd Kashdan, Maria Reiche, Valerie Thomas, Robert Biswas-Diener, John Flynn, Nadiya Hussain, Valentia Tereshkova, Maria Montessori

SCREENTiME

NOVA (TV), The Goonies, The Secret Garden, Mary Poppins Returns, Nadiya's British Food Adventure, Horrible Histories, Annedroids, Travel Shows with Ade Adepitan, Charlie and The Chocolate Factory

SONGS

Biscuits - Kacey Musgraves, If I Were A Boy- Beyoncé, Do I Wanna Know -The Arctic Monkeys, Fascination Street - The Cure, New Sensation - Inxs, Ask -The Smiths, A Cover is Not the Book- Mary Poppins Returns, Why - Annie Lennox, Spaceman- The Killers

TODAY'S DATE _____

MY STRETCH IT ANSWERS

MY SUPERSTARS

MY SCREEN TIME

MY SONGS LIST

EMPATHY

I KNOW WHEN MY FRiENDS ARE HAPPY OR SAD AND I HELP THEM.

Remember to check out the FUTR NOW **YouTube** Channel where all the Strengths SONGS listed in this book can be found in our handy STRENGTHS SONGS PLAYLISTS from Bravery to Zest. Find the YouTube links at futrnow.org

We'd love to hear your feedback. Please email here@futrnow.org with your suggestions for Superstars, Screentime and Songs!

EMPATHY

This person seems to always say just the right thing. This person shows empathy to a friend who is upset. OVERUSE =Over analysing. UNDERUSE = Clueless in social situations. IDEAL USE = Tuned in and savvy in social situations.

i) Write about a time when this strength really energised you. ii) List all the times/activities when you used this strength last week. iii) List what stopped you using this strength last week. iv) List ways you can use this strengths to overcome difficulties this week. Take one action today. v) Throughout your day PAUSE before you speak and act. Ask yourself, "Is what I'm about to do a reflection of who I am and what I want to be? Discuss each evening with a parent how it went.

Michelle Obama, Ellen DeGeneres, Graham Norton, Oprah Winfrey, Dacher Keltner, Jason Wachob, Lauren Lavern, Mike Leigh, Connie Britton, Daniel J. Siegel, Roman Krznaric, Spike Lee, George Orwell, Marshall Rosenberg, Alicia Keys, Tony Robbins, Shah Rukh Khan

Inside Out, We Bought A Zoo, The Dark Horse, Remember the Titans, Wonder, A Dog's Purpose, Gender Revolution, Elián, Your Name (Anime), Miss Kiet's Children, Driving Miss Daisy, Children of a Lesser God, I AM, 'I, Robot', Juno, Metallica: Some Kind of Monster, Once, Queen of Katwe, Erin Brockovich, My Left Foot, The Diving Bell & The Butterfly, The Immortal Life of Henrietta Lacks, The African Queen, An Education

SONGS

Vincent - Don McLean/Ed Sheeran cover, Let Me In - Alicia Keys, Borders - MIA, Merry Go Round - Kacey Musgraves, Eleanor Rigby- Beatles, Umbrella -Rihanna, Smile Like You Mean It - The Killers, Perfect Gentleman - Wyclef Jean, Common People - Pulp, Everybody Hurts - R.E.M, Living For The City - Stevie Wonder, The Gambler - Kenny Rogers, Everyday People - Mr Wendall, The People - Common

TODAY'S DATE _____

MY STRETCH IT ANSWERS

MY SUPERSTARS

MY SCREEN TIME

MY SONGS LIST

FAIRNESS

I TREAT PEOPLE THE WAY i LiKE TO BE TREATED.

Remember to check out the FUTR NOW **YouTube** Channel where all the Strengths SONGS listed in this book can be found in our handy STRENGTHS SONGS PLAYLISTS from Bravery to Zest. . Find the YouTube links at futrnow.org

We'd love to hear your feedback. Please email here@futrnow.org with your suggestions for Superstars, Screentime and Songs!

FAIRNESS

SPOT iT

This person resolves a dispute among family members by looking for and pointing out the common ground. This person includes someone in a group conversation who's usually left out. OVERUSE = Divisive Righteousness UNDERUSE = Prejudiced/Intolerant. IDEAL USE = Equal opportunity for all.

STRETCH iT

i) Write about a time when this strength really energised you. ii) List all the times/activities when you used this strength last week. iii) List what stopped you using this strength last week. iv) List ways you can use this strengths to overcome difficulties this week. Take one action today. v) Throughout your day PAUSE before you speak and act. Ask yourself, "Is what I'm about to do a reflection of who I am and what I want to be? Discuss each evening with a parent how it went.

SUPERSTARS

Nadia Murad, Colin Kaepernick, Amal Clooney, Shamsia Hassani, Yeonmi Park, Emma Watson, Eva Longoria, Sonita Alizadeh, Bradley Cooper, Serena Williams, Barack Obama, Licia Ronzulli, Billie Jean King, Ruby Nell Bridges, Emmeline Pankhurst

SCREENTiME

Gideon's Army, The Get Down (TV), Battle of The Sexes, Ai Weiwei: Never Sorry, Selma, Gandhi, Malcom X, Robin Hood: Prince of Thieves, To Kill A Mockingbird, X Men Films, Australia, Avatar, The Help, Milk

SONGS

Je Suis Chez Moi- Black M, Glory - John Legend & Common, Pride (In the Name of Love) - U2, Good Ol' Boys Club - Kacey Musgraves, I Kissed A Girl - Katy Perry, Freedom! '90 - George Michael, Take Me To Church - Hozier, Woman - Kesha feat The Dap Kings, Get Up Stand Up - Bob Marley , Freedom - Jimi Hendrix, Another Day In Paradise - Phil Collins

TODAY'S DATE _____

MY STRETCH iT ANSWERS

MY SUPERSTARS

MY SCREEN TiME

MY SONGS LiST

FORGiVENESS

I CAN LET iT GO WHEN A FRiEND MAKES MiSTAKES OR HURTS MY FEELiNGS.

Remember to check out the FUTR NOW **YouTube** Channel where all the Strengths SONGS listed in this book can be found in our handy STRENGTHS SONGS PLAYLISTS from Bravery to Zest. . Find the YouTube links at futrnow.org

We'd love to hear your feedback. Please email here@futrnow.org with your suggestions for Superstars, Screentime and Songs!

FORGIVENESS

SPOT iT

This person gives a friend a second chance. This person doesn't hold a grudge. This person moves on easily after arguments and lets it go. OVERUSE = Permissive. UNDERUSE = Merciless. IDEAL USE = Letting go of hurt when wronged

STRETCH iT

i) Write about a time when this strength really energised you. ii) List all the times/activities when you used this strength last week. iii) List what stopped you using this strength last week. iv) List ways you can use this strengths to overcome difficulties this week. Take one action today. v) Throughout your day PAUSE before you speak and act. Ask yourself, "Is what I'm about to do a reflection of who I am and what I want to be? Discuss each evening with a parent how it went.

SUPERSTARS

Desmond Tutu, Nelson Mandela, Immaculee Ilibagiza, Jennifer Hudson, Yoko Ono, Lucy Hone, John McCain

SCREENTiME

Andi Mack, The Chronicles of Narnia: The Lion, The Witch & the Wardrobe, Angela's Ashes, Les Miserables (Film), Flatliners, The Kids Are Alright (Film), Mind the Gap (Film), The Kite Runner

SONGS

Sorry - Justin Bieber, Hello -Adele, Unforgiven – Metallica, Famous Blue Raincoat - Leonard Cohen, These Days - Rudimental feat Jess Glynn, No Need To Argue- The Cranberries, Je Te Pardonne - Maître Gims & Sia, Forgive Them Father - Lauryn Hill, Learn To Let Go - Kesha, Sorry Seems To Be The Hardest Word - Elton John, I Don't Want to Fight - Tina Turner, Music When The Light Goes Out - The Libertines, Let it Be - Beatles

TODAY'S DATE _____

MY STRETCH iT ANSWERS

MY SUPERSTARS

MY SCREEN TiME

MY SONGS LiST

GRATITUDE

I'M THANKFUL FOR GOOD THINGS IN MY LIFE.

Remember to check out the FUTR NOW **YouTube** Channel where all the Strengths SONGS listed in this book can be found in our handy STRENGTHS SONGS PLAYLISTS from Bravery to Zest. . Find the YouTube links at futrnow.org

We'd love to hear your feedback. Please email here@futrnow.org with your suggestions for Superstars, Screentime and Songs!

GRATITUDE

SPOT iT

This person frequently says thank you. This person expresses thanks to others easily. This person tells others how much they are appreciated. This person recognises how fortunate they are to be breathing, eating, walking etc. OVERUSE = False flattery. UNDERUSE = Harsh individualism. IDEAL USE = Thankfulness for big and small things.

STRETCH iT

i) Write about a time when this strength really energised you. ii) List all the times/activities when you used this strength last week. iii) List what stopped you using this strength last week. iv) List ways you can use this strengths to overcome difficulties this week. Take one action today. v) Throughout your day PAUSE before you speak and act. Ask yourself, "Is what I'm about to do a reflection of who I am and what I want to be? Discuss each evening with a parent how it went.

SUPERSTARS

Oprah Winfrey, Steven Spielberg, Dwayne Johnson, Molly Hahn, Daniel Radcliffe, Goldie Hawn, Janice Kaplan, Robert A Emmons, Lauren Tober, Violeta Parra, Rigoberta Menchu Tum, Dominik Spenst, Lori Deschene, Thomas Gilovich

SCREENTiME

Groundhog Day, It's a Wonderful Life, The Colour Purple, Mrs Doubtfire, Life Is Beautiful, Lion, Can You Dig This?, Secret Millionaire (TV), Amélie

SONGS

Good Old Days - Keisha & Macklemore, Ain't Got No, I Got Life - Nina Simone, Grateful: Beyond the Lights - Rita Ora, Nothing Without You - The Weeknd, Thank you - Dido, Thank U - Alanis Morrissette, Three Little Birds - Bob Marley, Thank You - Kehlani, Video - India Arie, Fighter -Christina Aguilera, Thank U, next - Ariana Grande, Gracias a la Vida - Violeta Parra, What a Wonderful World - Louis Armstrong, , You're the Best Thing About Me - U2, Guitars & Cadillacs - Dwight Yoakam, My Favourite Things - Julie Andrews, Blessings - Tom Walker

TODAY'S DATE _____

MY STRETCH iT ANSWERS

MY SUPERSTARS

MY SCREEN TiME

MY SONGS LiST

Remember to check out the FUTR NOW **YouTube** Channel where all the Strengths SONGS listed in this book can be found in our handy STRENGTHS SONGS PLAYLISTS from Bravery to Zest. . Find the YouTube links at futrnow.org

We'd love to hear your feedback. Please email here@futrnow.org with your suggestions for Superstars, Screentime and Songs!

HONESTY

SPOT iT

This person shares private information about self easily and is is open about their intentions and opinions. This person gives valuable feedback even if it is negative. OVERUSE = Harsh or Rude. UNDERUSE = Fake. IDEAL USE = Being one hundred percent oneself, being authentic.

STRETCH iT

i) Write about a time when this strength really energised you. ii) List all the times/activities when you used this strength last week. iii) List what stopped you using this strength last week. iv) List ways you can use this strengths to overcome difficulties this week. Take one action today. v) Throughout your day PAUSE before you speak and act. Ask yourself, "Is what I'm about to do a reflection of who I am and what I want to be? Discuss each evening with a parent how it went.

SUPERSTARS

Gabi Wilson (HER), India Arie, Kristen Stewart, Kacey Musgraves, Prince Harry, Jessica Alba, Salma Heyak, Tupac Shakur, Bob Marley, Hayden Panettiere, Kate Middleton, Emma Thompson, Drew Barrymore, Nellie Bly, Professor Green, Kim Gordon, Ellen DeGeneres, Dwight Yoakam

SCREENTiME

Dis(Honesty): The Truth About Lies, The Wonder Years (TV), Supergirl (TV), My So Called Life, Veronica Mars, Casablanca, High School Musical Films, The Big Sleep, Corpse Bride, Superman: The Movie, On The Waterfront, Erin Brokovic, Patch Adams, Lincoln, A Few Good Men

SONGS

Monster - Eminem & Rihanna, Faking it - Kehlani & Calvin Harris, Focus - H.E.R., Thursday - Jess Glynne, Cry Baby - Paloma Faith, Sad But True - Metallica, It Wasn't Me - Shaggy, Ghetto Gospel - Tupac, Honesty - Billy Joel, Fake Tales of San Francisco - Arctic Monkeys, Heart of Glass - Blondie, On The Level - Leonard Cohen, Say Something - Justin Timberlake, Boys Don't Cry -The Cure, Real Situation - Bob Marley & The Wailers, Look Me In The Heart -Tina Turner

TODAY'S DATE _____

MY STRETCH IT ANSWERS

MY SUPERSTARS

MY SCREEN TIME

MY SONGS LIST

HOPE

I BELIEVE GOOD THINGS WILL HAPPEN. I SET LOTS OF GOALS.

Remember to check out the FUTR NOW **YouTube** Channel where all the Strengths SONGS listed in this book can be found in our handy STRENGTHS SONGS PLAYLISTS from Bravery to Zest. . Find the YouTube links at futrnow.org

We'd love to hear your feedback. Please email here@futrnow.org with your suggestions for Superstars, Screentime and Songs!

HOPE

SPOT iT

This person speaks about their goals and what they are working towards. This person sees the glass half-full. This person shifts the conversation to the best possible scenario and positive outcomes. OVERUSE = Blindly optimistic. UNDERUSE = Negativity. IDEAL USE = positive expectations

STRETCH iT

i) Write about a time when this strength really energised you. ii) List all the times/activities when you used this strength last week. iii) List what stopped you using this strength last week. iv) List ways you can use this strengths to overcome difficulties this week. Take one action today. v) Throughout your day PAUSE before you speak and act. Ask yourself, "Is what I'm about to do a reflection of who I am and what I want to be? Discuss each evening with a parent how it went.

SUPERSTARS

Lauren Potter, Johanna Nordblad, Melanie Lynch, Charlize Theron, Nick Vujicic, Sean Swarner, Lilian Bland, Martin Seligman, Yoko Ono, Nadine Gordimer, Sander Lak, Randy Pausch, Liz Murray, Jennifer Lopez, Lorena Ochoa, Florence Chadwick

SCREENTiME

Before The Flood, Sunshine Cleaning, The Impossible, Babe, ET: The Extra-Terrestrial, The Wizard of Oz, Miracle on 34th Street, The Sound of Music, Awakenings, Happy Go Lucky, Milk, The Wizard of Oz

SONGS

I Gotta Feeling - Black Eyed Peas, Keep Ya Head Up- Tupac, Here Comes the Sun - The Beatles, Bounce- Calvin Harris & Kelis, Happy - Pharrell Williams, Everything is Everything - Lauryn Hill, Rainbow - Kacey Musgraves, Dog Days Are Over - Florence & The Machine, Freedom - Beyonce & Kendrick Lamar, The Good Old Days- The Libertines, Feeling Good -Nina Simone, Rainbow – Kesha, Hope - Jaden Smith, Sun is Shining - Bob Marley & The Wailers, Don't Let The Sun Go Down On Me - Elton John, A Change is Gonna Come - Sam Cooke, Leave The Light On - Tom Walker

TODAY'S DATE _____

MY STRETCH iT ANSWERS

MY SUPERSTARS

MY SCREEN TiME

MY SONGS LiST

HUMILITY

NO BIGGIE!

I QUIETLY SHOW PEOPLE WHAT I CAN DO INSTEAD OF BRAGGING.

Remember to check out the FUTR NOW **YouTube** Channel where all the Strengths SONGS listed in this book can be found in our handy STRENGTHS SONGS PLAYLISTS from Bravery to Zest. . Find the YouTube links at futrnow.org

We'd love to hear your feedback. Please email here@futrnow.org with your suggestions for Superstars, Screentime and Songs!

HUMiLiTY

SPOT iT

This person spends more time listening to others than trying to add their own views. This person applauds the group effort. This person doesn't boast about their own achievements. OVERUSE = To belittle oneself - Self-deprecation. UNDERUSE = Conceited, Arrogant. IDEAL USE = Acting from the stance that achievement does not elevate your worth.

STRETCH iT

i) Write about a time when this strength really energised you. ii) List all the times/activities when you used this strength last week. iii) List what stopped you using this strength last week. iv) List ways you can use this strengths to overcome difficulties this week. Take one action today. v) Throughout your day PAUSE before you speak and act. Ask yourself, "Is what I'm about to do a reflection of who I am and what I want to be? Discuss each evening with a parent how it went.

SUPERSTARS

Maryam Mirzakhani, Jimmy Chin, Rosalind Franklin, Keanu Reeves, Adele, Jennifer Lawrence, Jonas Salk, Rafael Nadal, Annie Lennox, Carey Mulligan, Ed Sheeran, Seth Godwin, Eddie Redmayne

SCREENTiME

Batman, Gandhi, Spider Man, Super Man, The Truman Show, Rain Man, All about Eve, Ghost Dog: The Way of the Samurai (Film), Hero, Kung Fu Panda 3, Tron: Legacy, The Truman Show, Unbreakable

SONGS

Love Yourself -Justin Bieber, Doo Wop - Lauryn Hill, Human - Rag 'n Bone Man & Calvin Harris, High Horse- Kacey Musgraves, Silent All Those Years - Tori Amos, Holy Grail - Jay Z & Beyonce, Mr Vain - Culture Beat, We Don't Need Another Hero - Tina Turner, Ego - Rag 'n Bone Man, Don't Be Shy - The Libertines, Humility -Gorillaz, Just A Girl - No Doubt

TODAY'S DATE _____

MY STRETCH iT ANSWERS

MY SUPERSTARS

MY SCREEN TiME

MY SONGS LiST

HUMOUR

I LIKE TO MAKE OTHERS SMILE AND LAUGH

Remember to check out the FUTR NOW **YouTube** Channel where all the Strengths SONGS listed in this book can be found in our handy STRENGTHS SONGS PLAYLISTS from Bravery to Zest. . Find the YouTube links at futrnow.org

We'd love to hear your feedback. Please email here@futrnow.org with your suggestions for Superstars, Screentime and Songs!

HUMOUR

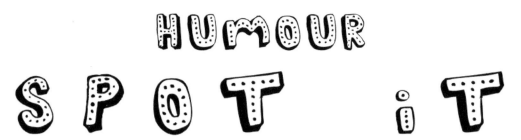

SPOT iT

This person tells jokes, funny stories and makes witty remarks in groups. This person teases or is playful with others one on one. OVERUSE = Giddiness. UNDERUSE = Staid, Serious. IDEAL USE = releasing tension with laughter, light heartedness.

STRETCH iT

i) Write about a time when this strength really energised you. ii) List all the times/activities when you used this strength last week. iii) List what stopped you using this strength last week. iv) List ways you can use this strengths to overcome difficulties this week. Take one action today. v) Throughout your day PAUSE before you speak and act. Ask yourself, "Is what I'm about to do a reflection of who I am and what I want to be? Discuss each evening with a parent how it went.

SUPERSTARS

Jim Carrey, David Walliams, Mindy Kaling, Amy Schumer, Matt Groening, Cameron Diaz, Michael McIntyre, Tom Shadyac, Tina Fey, Alex Turner, French & Saunders, Marilyn Monroe, Jim Davis, Melissa McCarty, Ben Stiller, Kate McKinnon, Will Ferrell, Wanda Sykes, Will Smith, Margaret Cho, Jack Black, Owen Wilson, Amy Poehler, Johnny Lever

SCREENTiME

The Monkees, Just Kidding, Corpse Bride, Ghostbusters (2016), Teen Titans Go! To the Movies, Life is Beautiful, Elf, The Tick (TV), Mouse Hunt, Ferris Bueller's Day Off, Tom & Jerry, Animaniacs, That 70s Show, Despicable Me, Patch Adams, Best in Show, Parenthood, The Odd Couple, Dumb & Dumber, Dodgeball: A True Underdog Story, Wallace & Gromit Films, Diary of a Wimpy Kid, Some Like It Hot

SONGS

Bug A Boo- Destinys Child, I Bet You Look On The Dance Floor- Arctic Monkeys, Smells like Nirvana - Weird Al Yankovic, Always Look on The Bright Side of Life - Monty Python, Peaches - The Presidents Of The United States of America, It Wasn't Me -Shaggy, Ob-La-Di Ob-La-Da - Beatles, The Monkees - Theme tune, Swish Swish - Katy Perry

TODAY'S DATE _____

MY STRETCH iT ANSWERS

MY SUPERSTARS

MY SCREEN TiME

MY SONGS LiST

Remember to check out the FUTR NOW **YouTube** Channel where all the Strengths SONGS listed in this book can be found in our handy STRENGTHS SONGS PLAYLISTS from Bravery to Zest. . Find the YouTube links at futrnow.org

We'd love to hear your feedback. Please email here@futrnow.org with your suggestions for Superstars, Screentime and Songs!

JUDGEMENT

SPOT iT

This person shares a new point of view each time when solving problems. This person often disagrees with a core idea, giving reasons and evidence against it. OVERUSE = Narrow-minded. UNDERUSE = Unreflective. IDEAL USE = Clear, open-mined, sensible thinking.

STRETCH iT

i) Write about a time when this strength really energised you. ii) List all the times/activities when you used this strength last week. iii) List what stopped you using this strength last week. iv) List ways you can use this strengths to overcome difficulties this week. Take one action today. v) Throughout your day PAUSE before you speak and act. Ask yourself, "Is what I'm about to do a reflection of who I am and what I want to be? Discuss each evening with a parent how it went.

SUPERSTARS

Sonia Sotomayor, Judge Ruth Bader Ginsburg, Spike Lee, Ludwig Guttman, Craig Revel Horwood, Alicia Keys, Emma Thompson, Virginia Hall, Patrick Stewart, Michelle Williams (Actress), Mary Warnock, Gloria Steinem, Elena Kagan

SCREENTiME

Steven Universe, Danger Mouse, Star Trek (The Next Generation TV), Spy Kids Films, RBG (Film), The Hounds of the Baskervilles, To Kill A Mockingbird, The Lady In The Van, The Boy In The Striped Panamas, A League of Their Own, Coco, Mouse Hunt

SONGS

Only God Can Judge Me - Tupac, Think For Yourself -The Beatles, Both Sides of the Story - Phil Collins, Fly Or Die- N.E.R.D., Think - Aretha Franklin, Church Of The Poison Mind- Culture Club, Free Your Mind - En Vogue, Mmmm - The Crash Test Dummies, Born This Way - Lady Gaga

TODAY'S DATE _____

MY STRETCH iT ANSWERS

MY SUPERSTARS

MY SCREEN TiME

MY SONGS LiST

KINDNESS

I LiKE TO DO NiCE THiNGS FOR OTHERS

Remember to check out the FUTR NOW **YouTube** Channel where all the Strengths SONGS listed in this book can be found in our handy STRENGTHS SONGS PLAYLISTS from Bravery to Zest. . Find the YouTube links at futrnow.org

We'd love to hear your feedback. Please email here@futrnow.org with your suggestions for Superstars, Screentime and Songs!

KINDNESS
SPOT iT

This person goes out of their way to help someone having a tough time. This person makes tea or helps others without being asked to. This person speaks respectful and pleasantly to others, no matter who they are. OVERUSE = Intrusiveness. UNDERUSE = Indifference. IDEAL USE = Doing things for others, small and big.

STRETCH iT

i) Write about a time when this strength really energised you. ii) List all the times/activities when you used this strength last week. iii) List what stopped you using this strength last week. iv) List ways you can use this strengths to overcome difficulties this week. Take one action today. v) Throughout your day PAUSE before you speak and act. Ask yourself, "Is what I'm about to do a reflection of who I am and what I want to be? Discuss each evening with a parent how it went.

SUPERSTARS

Nadia Comaneci, Giusi Nicolini, Temple Grandin, Elton John, Mursal Hedayat, Kristin Neff, Dalia Lama, Angelina Jolie, John Green, James Harrison, Khoudia Diop, Audrey Hepburn, Corrie ten Boom

SCREENTiME

Zoe Valentine, Glee, The Dragon Prince, Degrassi (TV), The Fresh Prince of Bel-Air, Andi Mack, Amelie, Wonder Woman Film, Napoleon Dynamite, Charlie and The Chocolate Factory (2005), A Christmas Carol (2009), How The Grinch Stole Christmas (2000), The Grinch, In This Corner Of The World (Anime 2016)

SONGS

Mercy - Duffy, Rude - Magic!, Don't Be So Hard On Yourself - Jess Glynne, Kill Em with Kindness - Selena Gomez, Unconditional Love - Tupac, Try a Little Kindness - Glenn Campbell/Brad Paisley Humble & Kind - Tim McGraw, Brothers Keeper – India Arie, I'll Stand By You - The Pretenders, Stand By Me- Ben E. King/John Lennon

TODAY'S DATE _____

MY STRETCH iT ANSWERS

MY SUPERSTARS

MY SCREEN TiME

MY SONGS LiST

LEADERSHIP

I LIKE TO TELL OTHERS HOW THEY CAN GET THINGS DONE.

Remember to check out the FUTR NOW **YouTube** Channel where all the Strengths SONGS listed in this book can be found in our handy STRENGTHS SONGS PLAYLISTS from Bravery to Zest. . Find the YouTube links at futrnow.org

We'd love to hear your feedback. Please email here@futrnow.org with your suggestions for Superstars, Screentime and Songs!

LEADERSHIP

SPOT iT

This person organises a get-together among friends. This person inspires other's with their vision. This person motivates others to follow and rally behind a cause/idea. OVERUSE = Despotism. UNDERUSE = Compliant. IDEAL USE. = Positively influencing others

STRETCH iT

i) Write about a time when this strength really energised you. ii) List all the times/activities when you used this strength last week. iii) List what stopped you using this strength last week. iv) List ways you can use this strengths to overcome difficulties this week. Take one action today. v) Throughout your day PAUSE before you speak and act. Ask yourself, "Is what I'm about to do a reflection of who I am and what I want to be? Discuss each evening with a parent how it went.

SUPERSTARS

Greta Thunberg, Leymah Gbowee, Sophie Scholl, Alyssa Milano, Malala Yousafzai, Melinda Gates, Mahatma Gandhi, Alexandria Ocasio-Cortez, Al Gore, Ban Ki Moon, Mark Williamson (Action for Happiness), Sally Ride, Jamie Oliver, Lea Waters , Angela Merkel, Simone Veil, Eleanor Roosevelt, Steve Jobs, Deepak Chopra, Anita Roddick

SCREENTiME

Lawrence of Arabia, Star Trek: The First Contact, He Named Me Malala, The Kings Speech, Girl Rising, Avatar, Moana, The Lion King, Ben Hur (Film 1959), Apollo 13, Dances With Wolves, Gandhi, Glory (Film 1989), High Noon (Film 1952) An Inconvenient Truth, An Inconvenient Sequel, The Lion King, Spartacus (Film 1960)

SONGS

Girl On Fire - Alicia Keys, Run The World (Girls) - Beyoncé, Pray for Me - The Weeknd & Kendrick Lamar, Fall in Line - Christina Aguilera & Demi Levato, Independent Women, Pt. 1 - Destiny's Child, Follow Your Arrow - Kacey Musgraves, Unstoppable - Sia, Confident - Demi Lovato, Can't Get Enough Of Myself - Santigold, Doubt - Mary J. Blige, Fight Song - Rachel Platten, Most Girls - Hailee Steinfeld, Never Give Up - Sia, Step By Step - Whitney Houston, The Champion - Carrie Underwood

TODAY'S DATE _____

MY STRETCH iT ANSWERS

MY SUPERSTARS

MY SCREEN TiME

MY SONGS LiST

LOVE

I TELL PEOPLE I
LOVE THEM.
I MiSS THEM
WHEN THEY ARE
NOT AROUND.

Remember to check out the FUTR NOW **YouTube** Channel where all the Strengths SONGS listed in this book can be found in our handy STRENGTHS SONGS PLAYLISTS from Bravery to Zest. . Find the YouTube links at futrnow.org

We'd love to hear your feedback. Please email here@futrnow.org with your suggestions for Superstars, Screentime and Songs!

LOVE SPOT iT

This person express warmth, affection, genuineness and attentive listening with good eye contact when talking to others. This person is tactile and often hugs others. OVERUSE = Expressing love to everyone, even if it's not mutual. UNDERUSE = Emotionally detached and disconnected. IDEAL USE = Showing genuine warmth towards others.

STRETCH iT

i) Write about a time when this strength really energised you. ii) List all the times/activities when you used this strength last week. iii) List what stopped you using this strength last week. iv) List ways you can use this strengths to overcome difficulties this week. Take one action today. v) Throughout your day PAUSE before you speak and act. Ask yourself, "Is what I'm about to do a reflection of who I am and what I want to be? Discuss each evening with a parent how it went.

SUPERSTARS

John and Julie Gottman, John Legend, Gustaf Klimt, Robert Indiana, Alicia Keys, Barbara Fredrickson, Goldie Hawn, Sting and Trudy Styler, Gilbert Baker, John Lennon and Yoko Ono, Patrick Stewart, Matthew Kaplan (Be One), Walt Whitman

SCREENTiME

Truly Madly Deeply, Love Simon, Casablanca, Iris, Life is Beautiful, Monsoon Wedding, Shakespeare in Love, Roman Holiday, Harry Potter Films

SONGS

Mama - Clean Bandits & Ellie Goulding, Make Me Feel Janelle - Monáe, Sweet Child Of Mine- G 'n R, Dear Mama -Tupac, Make You Feel My Love - Adele, Rockabye - Clean Bandit, Feels- Calvin Harris, Could You Be Loved - Bob Marley, Nothing Breaks Like A Heart - Mark Ronson & Miley Cyrus, The Greatest Love of All - Whitney Houston, Walk Alone - Rudimental/Tom Walker, You Got The Love - Florence & The Machine, I'll Be There - Jess Glynne, Love's in Need of Love Today-Stevie Wonder, Where is The Love -The Black Eyed Peas, All You Need is Love - The Beatles,

TODAY'S DATE _____

MY STRETCH IT ANSWERS

MY SUPERSTARS

MY SCREEN TIME

MY SONGS LIST

LOVE OF LEARNING

I LIKE LEARNING NEW THINGS WHEREVER I GO.

Remember to check out the FUTR NOW **YouTube** Channel where all the Strengths SONGS listed in this book can be found in our handy STRENGTHS SONGS PLAYLISTS from Bravery to Zest. . Find the YouTube links at futrnow.org

We'd love to hear your feedback. Please email here@futrnow.org with your suggestions for Superstars, Screentime and Songs!

LOVE OF LEARNING

SPOT iT

This person carries a book around with them wherever they go, reading on their breaks. This person tries new things, signing up for new courses in varied subjects. OVERUSE = Know-it-all. UNDERUSE = Complacency, not bothered. IDEAL USE = Organised deepening of knowledge

STRETCH iT

i) Write about a time when this strength really energised you. ii) List all the times/activities when you used this strength last week. iii) List what stopped you using this strength last week. iv) List ways you can use this strengths to overcome difficulties this week. Take one action today. v) Throughout your day PAUSE before you speak and act. Ask yourself, "Is what I'm about to do a reflection of who I am and what I want to be? Discuss each evening with a parent how it went.

SUPERSTARS

Mikhail Baryshnikov, Rory Charles Graham, Maya Gabeira, Julia Child, Elon Musk, Maureen Gaffney, Dave Grohl, Adam Lowry, Bruce Dickinson, Georgia O'Keeffe, Matt Smith, Reese Witherspoon, James Franco, Willie Nelson, Michael Jordan, Kylie Minogue, James Corden, Prince, Gwen Stefani, Sal Khan, Mihaly Csikszentmihalyi

SCREENTiME

BBC Newsround, Wild Kratts, CBBC Book Club, Planet Earth, School Of Rock, Zootopia, Dead Poet's Society, Blue Peter, Billy Elliot, Julie & Julia, Khan Academy, Vsauce, SciShow, BBC Learning Zone, Eat Pray Love, Life Animated, Harry Potter 5 – Order of the Phoenix

SONGS

Jump - Madonna, Starting Over - John Lennon, Growing up - Macklemore & Ryan Lewis, The Climb - Miley Cyrus, Try Everything- Shakira, Absolute Beginners - David Bowie, Dancing - Kylie, Learning to Fly - Tom Petty, School's Out -Alice Cooper, Learning The Game - Buddy Holly, Learn To Fly - Foo Fighters

TODAY'S DATE _____

MY STRETCH IT ANSWERS

MY SUPERSTARS

MY SCREEN TIME

MY SONGS LIST

PERSERVERANCE

I DON'T GIVE UP EASILY. I TRY AND TRY AND TRY.

Remember to check out the FUTR NOW **YouTube** Channel where all the Strengths SONGS listed in this book can be found in our handy STRENGTHS SONGS PLAYLISTS from Bravery to Zest. . Find the YouTube links at futrnow.org

We'd love to hear your feedback. Please email here@futrnow.org with your suggestions for Superstars, Screentime and Songs!

PERSEVERANCE

SPOT iT

This person sees tasks through even when others want to give up. This person finishes projects on time and receives certificates and awards for their accomplishments. OVERUSE = Obsessiveness. UNDERUSE = Quitter, Fragility. IDEAL USE = Persisting to overcome obstacles.

STRETCH iT

i) Write about a time when this strength really energised you. ii) List all the times/activities when you used this strength last week. iii) List what stopped you using this strength last week. iv) List ways you can use this strengths to overcome difficulties this week. Take one action today. v) Throughout your day PAUSE before you speak and act. Ask yourself, "Is what I'm about to do a reflection of who I am and what I want to be? Discuss each evening with a parent how it went.

SUPERSTARS

Poorna Malavath, Hillary Clinton, Jessica Ennis, Alicia Alonso, Lowri Morgan, Virginia Hall, Ellen MacArthur, Michael Phelps, Beatrice Vio, Paula Radcliffe, Jimmy Chin, Steven Hawking, Mo Farah, Fridtjof Nansen, Stevie Wonder, Michael "Eddie the Eagle" Edwards, Dorothy Hodgkin

SCREENTiME

Firefly, Scooby-Doo, Where Are You! Magnus, Anne with an E, Strictly Come Dancing, First Position, Touching the Void, A Wrinkle in Time, Chariots of Fire, Gone with the Wind, 2001 A Space Odyssey, The Karate Kid, Eddie The Eagle, Everest, Forrest Gump, The Grapes of Wrath, The Colour Purple, The Pianist, Moana

SONGS

Skyfall - Adele, Formation - Beyoncé, I'm Still Standing - Elton John, All the Stars - Kendrick Lamar & SZA, One Way Or Another - Blondie, Never Say Never - Justin Bieber, My Silver Lining - First Aid Kit, Harder Better Faster Stronger -Daft Punk, Rewrite The Stars - Anne Marie & James Arthur, Running Up That Hill- Kate Bush, Walk On - U2, I Won't Back Down - Tom Petty, The Show Must Go On - Queen, Alive - Pearl Jam, When the Levee Breaks - Led Zeppelin, Hang onto Your Love - Sade, Try - Pink

TODAY'S DATE _____

MY STRETCH iT ANSWERS

MY SUPERSTARS

MY SCREEN TiME

MY SONGS LiST

POINT OF VIEW

I GIVE GOOD ADVICE TO THE PEOPLE IN MY LIFE.

 Perspective in VIA*

Remember to check out the FUTR NOW **YouTube** Channel where all the Strengths SONGS listed in this book can be found in our handy STRENGTHS SONGS PLAYLISTS from Bravery to Zest. . Find the YouTube links at futrnow.org

We'd love to hear your feedback. Please email here@futrnow.org with your suggestions for Superstars, Screentime and Songs!

SPOT iT

This person gives practical advice to friends. This person comments on the bigger picture of a topic and notices the wider impact to humanity. OVERUSE = Overbearing. UNDERUSE = Shallowness. IDEAL USE = Sees the bigger picture

STRETCH iT

i) Write about a time when this strength really energised you. ii) List all the times/activities when you used this strength last week. iii) List what stopped you using this strength last week. iv) List ways you can use this strengths to overcome difficulties this week. Take one action today. v) Throughout your day PAUSE before you speak and act. Ask yourself, "Is what I'm about to do a reflection of who I am and what I want to be? Discuss each evening with a parent how it went.

SUPERSTARS

Sara Seagar, Eufrosina Cruz, Rachel Carson, Ava Marie DuVernay, Bob Geldof, Mary Shelley, Bono, Tim Berners Lee, Maria Montessori, Jessica Alba, Jamie Oliver, J.J. Abrams, Tupac Shakur, Pablo Picasso, James Cameron, Brenda Chapman, The Mirabel Sisters, Leonardo DiCaprio, Elizabeth Kolbert, Black M.

SCREENTiME

Living On One Dollar, More Than Honey, Tales By Light, BBC Newsround, Who Do You Think You Are?, Zootopia, Napoleon Dynamite, Star Wars Films, Lord of The Rings, Karate Kid, The Kid, To Kill a Mockingbird, Sliding Doors

SONGS

In This Together – Ellie Goulding, Meme - Maître Gims & Vianney, Rainbow - Kacey Musgraves, Chained To The Rhythm - Katy Perry, Big Picture - London Grammar, Feed The World - Bob Geldof, One Point Perspective - Arctic Monkeys, Nevermind - Nirvana, One Love - Bob Marley, Watching The Wheels - John Lennon, Toast To Our Differences - Rudimental, Eyes Open - Taylor Swift, Parallel Universe - Red Hot Chilli Peppers, Days Like This - Van Morrison, One - U2

TODAY'S DATE _____

MY STRETCH IT ANSWERS

MY SUPERSTARS

MY SCREEN TIME

MY SONGS LIST

PRUDENCE

I AM CAREFUL TO NOT TAKE TOO MANY RISKS.

Remember to check out the FUTR NOW **YouTube** Channel where all the Strengths SONGS listed in this book can be found in our handy STRENGTHS SONGS PLAYLISTS from Bravery to Zest. . Find the YouTube links at futrnow.org

We'd love to hear your feedback. Please email here@futrnow.org with your suggestions for Superstars, Screentime and Songs!

PRUDENCE

SPOT IT

This person keeps various folders and organisers. This person arrives on time or before the time. This person waits for all the information before making a decision. OVERUSE = Stick in the mud, pussy foot. UNDERUSE = Thrill seeker. IDEAL USE = Wise caution

STRETCH IT

i) Write about a time when this strength really energised you. ii) List all the times/activities when you used this strength last week. iii) List what stopped you using this strength last week. iv) List ways you can use this strengths to overcome difficulties this week. Take one action today. v) Throughout your day PAUSE before you speak and act. Ask yourself, "Is what I'm about to do a reflection of who I am and what I want to be? Discuss each evening with a parent how it went.

SUPERSTARS

Katherine Johnson, Dorothy Vaughan, Mary Jackson, Sofia Ionescu, Margaret Hamilton, Boyan Slat, Sarah Jessica Parker, Kate Middleton, Ed Sheeran, Kendrick Lamar, Carrie Underwood, Dave Grohl, Stella Rimington

SCREENTIME

Driving Miss Daisy, The Queen, Sense and Sensibility, The Shawshank Redemption, Our Planet

SONGS

Jolene - Dolly Pardon/Miley Cyrus, Gwen Stefani - What You Waiting For?, Le Pire – Maitre Gims, Danger High Voltage- Electric Six, Tightrope - Janelle Monáe & Big Boi, What's Up Danger - Black Caviar, Don't Stop Me Now - Queen, Being Boring - Pet Shop Boys, Caution - Mariah Carey, Dear Prudence - The Beatles, Shelter From The Storm - Bob Dylan, Protection - Massive Attack, Caution - Damian Marley, Madonna - Hung Up

TODAY'S DATE _____
MY STRETCH iT ANSWERS

MY SUPERSTARS

MY SCREEN TiME

MY SONGS LiST

SELF-CONTROL

I WATCH WHAT I DO AND SAY.

 Self-Regulation in VIA*

Remember to check out the FUTR NOW **YouTube** Channel where all the Strengths SONGS listed in this book can be found in our handy STRENGTHS SONGS PLAYLISTS from Bravery to Zest. . Find the YouTube links at futrnow.org

We'd love to hear your feedback. Please email here@futrnow.org with your suggestions for Superstars, Screentime and Songs!

SELF-CONTROL

This person goes for a run/walk everyday. The person goes to bed on time without being asked. The person makes healthy food choices like salad and fruit. OVERUSE = Inhibition. UNDERUSE = Self-indulgence. IDEAL USE = Self-management of vices.

i) Write about a time when this strength really energised you. ii) List all the times/activities when you used this strength last week. iii) List what stopped you using this strength last week. iv) List ways you can use this strengths to overcome difficulties this week. Take one action today. v) Throughout your day PAUSE before you speak and act. Ask yourself, "Is what I'm about to do a reflection of who I am and what I want to be? Discuss each evening with a parent how it went.

Arianna Huffington, Valentina Tereshkova, Louis Smith, Uma Thurman, Samantha Cristoforetti, Sting, Martina Navratilova, Grace Hopper, Chris Hatfield, Jiro Ono, Marie Kondo, Shaun Thompson, Hrithik Roshan, Kino McGregor, Amir Iqbal Khan, Shaun Thompson, Bruce Lee

A Star Is Born, Crazy Rich Asians, Girlfight, Rocky, Focus:T25, Kino McGregor YouTube, Family Ties, Supergirl, Ralph Breaks the Internet, Inside Out, Forest Gump, The Bridge on the River Kwai, Twilight, Black Swan, Bourne Identity, The Maltese Falcon, Man on a Wire, The Queen

Chandelier - Sia, Stop - Justice, Gangsta - Kehlani, Stop Your Sobbing - The Pretenders, St Anger - Metallica, Clean Up Time - John Lennon, In For The Kill - La Roux, Til I'm Done - Paloma Faith, King - Years & Years, She's Lost Control - Joy Division, Under the Bridge – Red Hot Chili Peppers, True Faith - New Order, You Know I'm No Good - Amy Winehouse, Walk the Line-Johnny Cash, The Man Who Sold The World – David Bowie/Nirvana, Don't Go - Yaz, I Love To Hate You - Erasure, Love Is A Stanger - Eurythmics

TODAY'S DATE _____

MY STRETCH iT ANSWERS

MY SUPERSTARS

MY SCREEN TiME

MY SONGS LiST

SPiRiTUALiTY

I THiNK ABOUT LiFE AND HOW EVERYTHiNG iS CONNECTED.

Remember to check out the FUTR NOW **YouTube** Channel where all the Strengths SONGS listed in this book can be found in our handy STRENGTHS SONGS PLAYLISTS from Bravery to Zest. . Find the YouTube links at futrnow.org

We'd love to hear your feedback. Please email here@futrnow.org with your suggestions for Superstars, Screentime and Songs!

SPIRITUALITY

SPOT iT

This person spends break times in quiet reflection, contemplation, meditation or prayer. This person can see beyond what is happening now to a higher connection or meaning. This person can connect to a deeper purpose of a situation. OVERUSE = Fanaticism, UNDERUSE = purposeless life, IDEAL USE = Connecting and respecting ALL beings to find meaning in life.

STRETCH iT

i) Write about a time when this strength really energised you. ii) List all the times/activities when you used this strength last week. iii) List what stopped you using this strength last week. iv) List ways you can use this strengths to overcome difficulties this week. Take one action today. v) Throughout your day PAUSE before you speak and act. Ask yourself, "Is what I'm about to do a reflection of who I am and what I want to be? Discuss each evening with a parent how it went.

SUPERSTARS

Deepak Chopra, Tiber Hawkeye, Jon Kabat Zinn, Sadhguru, Elizabeth Mattis-Namgyel, Thich Nhat Hanh, Pema Chödrön, Jack Kornfield, Arianna Huffington, Matthieu Ricard, Ram Dass, Arianna Huffington, Yoko Ono, Viktor Frankl

SCREENTiME

Avatar: The Last Airbender, Big Fish & Begonia, 2001: A Space Odyssey, The Incredibles, Field of Dreams, The Chronicles of Narnia, Gandhi, Run Lola Run, The Wizard of Oz, Seven Years in Tibet, The Way, Indiana Jones Films, Salmon Fishing in the Yemen, Spirited Away

SONGS

Hymn - Kesha, Instant Karma - Plastic Ono Band, My Sweet Lord - George Harrison, Hymn of the Big Wheel - Massive Attack, Pray - Sam Smith, Jesus Walks - Kanye West, Human - Rag 'n Bone Man, I Still Haven't Found What I'm Looking For - U2, Praying for Time - George Michael, Imagine - John Lennon, God is A DJ - Faithless, Have A Talk With God - Stevie Wonder, In God's Country - U2, Redemption song - Bob Marley, Voodoo Child - Jimi Hendrix, Stairway To Heaven - Led Zeppelin, No Religion - Van Morrison, Human - The Killers

TODAY'S DATE _____

MY STRETCH iT ANSWERS

MY SUPERSTARS

MY SCREEN TiME

MY SONGS LiST

TEAMWORK

I LIKE TO WORK WITH MY FRIENDS

Remember to check out the FUTR NOW **YouTube** Channel where all the Strengths SONGS listed in this book can be found in our handy STRENGTHS SONGS PLAYLISTS from Bravery to Zest. . Find the YouTube links at futrnow.org

We'd love to hear your feedback. Please email here@futrnow.org with your suggestions for Superstars, Screentime and Songs!

This person asks the opinion of everyone on the team. This person chooses to work with others rather than alone. OVERUSE =   Dependent on others. UNDERUSE = Selfish. IDEAL USE = Collaborative and participating fully in groups

i) Write about a time when this strength really energised you. ii) List all the times/activities when you used this strength last week. iii) List what stopped you using this strength last week. iv) List ways you can use this strengths to overcome difficulties this week. Take one action today. v) Throughout your day PAUSE before you speak and act. Ask yourself, "Is what I'm about to do a reflection of who I am and what I want to be? Discuss each evening with a parent how it went.

Gerty and Carl Cori, Troop 6000, Sunrise Movement, The Beatles, The Black Mambas, Together for Yes, Bletchleyettes, Apollo 11 team, New Zealand All Blacks, USA women's soccer team (2015), Dorothy Vaughan, Maria Viera Da Silva, Laura & Kate Mulleavy

Hoop Dreams, The Gabby Douglas Story, Soul Surfer, The Summit, Metallica Some Kid of Monster , Rogue One: A Star Wars Story, Just Add Magic, Glitter Force Doki Doki, Little Miss Sunshine, March of the Penguins, Shrek Films, Grapes of Wrath, Cool Runnings, The African Queen, Toy Story, The Way Back

Skyfall - Adele, Lean On - DJ Snake & Major Lazer , We Are Your Friends - Justice & Simian, Giant- Calvin Harris & Rag'n Bone Man, Ghost Town - Madonna, Sometimes You Can't Make It On Your Own - U2, Team - Lorde, Back On The Chain Gang - Pretenders, Everything is Awesome - Lego Movie, Come Together -The Beatles, Can't Stand Me Now -The Libertines

TODAY'S DATE _____

MY STRETCH IT ANSWERS

MY SUPERSTARS

MY SCREEN TIME

MY SONGS LIST

WONDERMENT

I FEEL AWE SEEING SUPERB ART & MUSIC & NOTICING NATURE'S BEAUTY.

 Appreciation of Beauty in VIA*

Remember to check out the FUTR NOW **YouTube** Channel where all the Strengths SONGS listed in this book can be found in our handy STRENGTHS SONGS PLAYLISTS from Bravery to Zest. . Find the YouTube links at futrnow.org

We'd love to hear your feedback. Please email here@futrnow.org with your suggestions for Superstars, Screentime and Songs!

Printed by Amazon Italia Logistica S.r.l.
Torrazza Piemonte (TO), Italy

10184909R00063

Why not get other family members to complete the strengths survey too - you can share the link to the strengths survey here http://futrnow.pro.viasurvey.org

Write and draw in above your Strengths Family Tree, adding as many family members as you wish!

TODAY'S DATE _____

MY STRETCH IT ANSWERS

MY SUPERSTARS

MY SCREEN TIME

MY SONGS LIST

STRENGTHS FAMILY TREE

ZEST

SPOT iT

This person regularly walks or exercises on their breaks. This person spends money on experiences with friends rather than things. OVERUSE = Hyperactive. UNDERUSE = Sedentary, Lethargic. IDEAL USE = Enthusiasm for life.

STRETCH iT

i) Write about a time when this strength really energised you. ii) List all the times/activities when you used this strength last week. iii) List what stopped you using this strength last week. iv) List ways you can use this strengths to overcome difficulties this week. Take one action today. v) Throughout your day PAUSE before you speak and act. Ask yourself, "Is what I'm about to do a reflection of who I am and what I want to be? Discuss each evening with a parent how it went.

SUPERSTARS

Maddie Ziegler, Maya Gabeira, Beyonce, Deepika Padukone, Aishwarya Rai, Akram Khan, Carmen Amaya, Marco Borges, Shah Rukh Khan, Bruno Tonioli, Simone Biles, Lella Lombardi, Usain Bolt, Florence Griffith Joyner, Nicola Adams, Tara Stiles, Joe Wicks

SCREENTiME

Finding Neverland, Grease, Mary Poppins, Footloose, Bend It Like Beckham, Tara Stiles (You Tube), Joe Wicks School Fitness, Strictly Come Dancing (TV), Singing in the Rain, New York City Ballet (YouTube), The Royal Ballet (You Tube), The Sound of Music, National Velvet, I Am Bolt, Whip It, Buena Vista Social Club Taal, Rab ne bana de Jodi (Bollywood Film)

SONGS

Electricity - Calvin Harris & Dua Lipa, Outta Space -The Prodigy, Jumpin Jumpin- Destinys Child, Vogue - Madonna, Cheap Thrills - Sia & Sean Pau, Can't Hold Us - Macklemore, Pump Up The Jam - Technotronic, Let's Go Crazy - Prince, Shake it Off- Taylor Swift, Moves Like Jagger- Maroon 5 ,Firework - Katy Perry, Dancing In The Street - Martha & The Vandellas, Push it - Salt 'n Pepper, Running Free – Iron Maiden, Dance With Somebody - Whitney Houston, Movement – Hozier, Soni Soni - Mohabbatein

Remember to check out the FUTR NOW **YouTube** Channel where all the Strengths SONGS listed in this book can be found in our handy STRENGTHS SONGS PLAYLISTS from Bravery to Zest. . Find the YouTube links at futrnow.org

We'd love to hear your feedback. Please email here@futrnow.org with your suggestions for Superstars, Screentime and Songs!

ZEST

I HAVE LOTS OF ENERGY.

TODAY'S DATE _____
MY STRETCH IT ANSWERS

MY SUPERSTARS

MY SCREEN TIME

MY SONGS LIST

WONDERMENT

SPOT iT

This person gets excited about going to art museums, theatre, opera, concerts and cultural events. This person's room displays art on walls. The person is awe struck by sunsets, skyscrapers, guitar solos or interesting birds/animals. OVERUSE = Snobbery, perfectionism. UNDERUSE = Oblivious. IDEAL USE = Seeing the life behind things

STRETCH iT

i) Write about a time when this strength really energised you. ii) List all the times/activities when you used this strength last week. iii) List what stopped you using this strength last week. iv) List ways you can use this strengths to overcome difficulties this week. Take one action today. v) Throughout your day PAUSE before you speak and act. Ask yourself, "Is what I'm about to do a reflection of who I am and what I want to be? Discuss each evening with a parent how it went.

SUPERSTARS

Katia Krafft, Joan Bra, Maud Stevens Wagner, Gae Aulenti, Kevin McCloud, Annie Mac, Peggy Guggenheim, Vivian Maier, David Attenborough, WB Yeats, Naomi Shihab Nye, Maria Abramovic, Marie Tharp, David Hockney, Clara Rockmore, Gae Aulenti, Louise Bourgeois

SCREENTiME

Abstract: The Art of Design, Wild Kratts, Mountain, Flight of the Butterflies, Finding Vivian Maier, Floyd Norman: An Animated Life, Hidden Kingdoms, Blue Planet, Life, Louise Bourgeois: The Spider, the Mistress and the Tangerine, Crouching Tiger, Hidden Dragon, Amélie, The Soloist, Midnight in Paris, Tea with Mussolini, It's a Wonderful Life

SONGS

Champagne Supernova - Oasis, Waterloo Sunset - The Kinks, Ray Of Light – Madonna, Kelly Watch The Stars – Air, Wonder - Naughty Boy feat. Emeli Sandé, The Night Is Still Young - Nicki Minaj, Amazing - How Big How Blue How Beautiful- Florence & The Machine, A Forest - The Cure, Naked In The Rain - Blue Pearl, Albatross - Fleetwood Mac, The Moon - Cat Power, Graceland - Paul Simon